W9-CKC-033

THE GREAT CITY SEARCH

Rosie Heywood

Illustrated by David Hancock

Edited by Kamini Khanduri

Project designer: Russell Punter

Series editor: Felicity Brooks

Contents

Cover design: Helen Wood

About this book

Welcome to the City. You'll be spending the day with Mayor Maurice, and in the evening, you'll be going to the grand opening of the new City swimming pool. As you travel around, there are all kinds of things to find.

This is Mayor Maurice. He's made a list of the things he has to do today.

This map shows the places you will visit in the City.

Mayor Maurice says that in each place, you have to find someone who helped to get the new swimming pool ready, and invite them to the grand opening. But he's not sure which person is in which place – that's one of the puzzles for you to solve. Here's who you have to find:

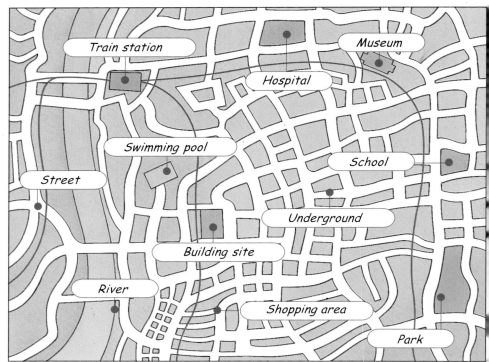

Train station
Museum
Hospital
Swimming pool
School
Street
Underground
Building site
River
Shopping area
Park

Paul the painter holding a paintbrush

Lucy the lifeguard with her towel

Bob the builder with a trowel

Asha the architect with her sketch pad

Pete the planner holding his plans

Pippa the photographer holding her camera

Jack the journalist holding his tape recorder

Ellie the electrician with her toolbox

Chuck the carpenter holding his saw

Pam the plumber holding a wrench

What to spot

Each of the double pages in this book shows a different place in the City. There are lots of things to look for in each place. Some things are easy to spot, but some are very tricky. This is how the puzzles work.

This strip tells you why Mayor Maurice has come to each place and how long he will spend there.

This tells you what Mayor Maurice is doing. You'll find him in every place.

These little pictures show the things you can find in the big picture.

The writing next to each little picture tells you how many of that thing to look for in the big picture.

This box is a reminder of the things that the people you have to find will be holding. There's one person in each place.

Even if you can only see part of a thing, it still counts.

This tells you to find something you'll need in the next place.

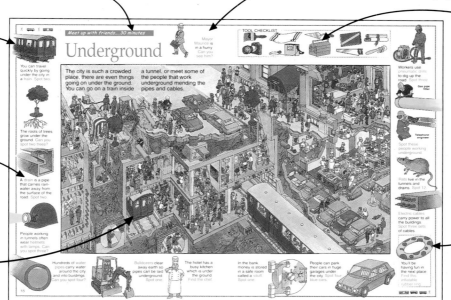

Finding the way

When you've done all the puzzles on a double page, you have to find out where to go next – it won't be the place on the next page in the book. You also need to find out how to travel there. Here's what you do.

In the bottom right-hand corner of each double page, four tiny pictures tell you how to travel to the next place.

To find out where to go next, look for exactly the same four pictures in the top left-hand corner of another double page.

You'll travel by underground train, taxi, bus, or on foot. But you won't use all these ways of getting around on each journey.

PUZZLE CHECKLIST

In each place, you must find:
* ★ Mayor Maurice
* ★ One person to invite to the grand opening
* ★ Lots of things hidden in the big picture
* ★ One thing you'll need in the next place
* ★ Which place to go to next

If you get stuck finding your way, there's a map showing the correct route on page 26. If you get stuck doing any of the other puzzles, you'll find all the answers on pages 28-31. Now turn the page to begin your Great City Search...

At the station

Information screens show what time trains arrive and leave. Spot nine.

There are plenty of clocks in the station. Can you find six?

Bags of mail often arrive in the City by train. Spot four trolleys full of mailbags.

Taxis take people from the station to other parts of the City. Find four.

You've arrived at the City railway station. It's full of bustling crowds and noise. Trains are arriving and leaving every few minutes. People are hurrying into the City or waiting for their train journeys to begin.

High speed trains can travel at over 250 km (155 miles) per hour. Spot one.

Can you spot 18 people with large backpacks?

Escalators take you to the trains that run underground. Can you see one going down?

TOOL CHECKLIST

Visitors go to the information desk to find out about the City. Find it.

Sandwich

Magazine

Flowers

You can shop while you wait for your train. Find where you can buy these things.

Cleaners use these cleaning machines to sweep the station floor. Spot three.

You're going shopping in the next place. Find this bag to put your things in.

Can you find this man who is running to catch his train?

You can buy tickets from an office or from a ticket machine. Find eight.

Conductors make sure the train doors are shut, and tell the driver when to leave. Spot six.

Mayor Maurice is just about to watch a video. Spot him.

Museum plans show you what to see in each room. Find four.

You can go on a museum tour with a guide. Can you spot five?

Greek vase

Egyptian sculpture

Some of the things are thousands of years old. Spot three of each of these.

Can you find this giant model of a butterfly?

In the museum

This huge museum is full of interesting things to look at. You can learn about animals from around the world and how people lived long ago. There is too much to see in one visit, so you will have to come back another day.

Bicycles called Penny Farthings were built in England over a hundred years ago. Spot one.

Museum curators study the objects and look after them. Find a curator using a microscope.

You can use these telephones and screens to get information. Can you spot 11?

Open the new display.....1 hour

TOOL CHECKLIST

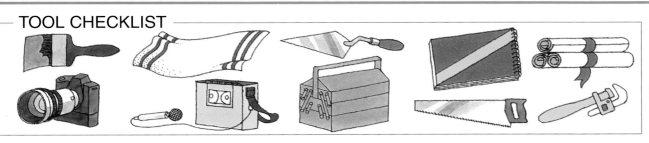

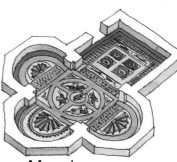

Mosaics are pictures made from tiny pieces of stone. Spot this Roman mosaic.

Pteranodon

Head of Tyrannosaurus rex

Triceratops

Huge models show you what dinosaurs might have looked like. Find each of these.

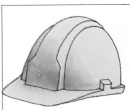

You can stop for a bite to eat at the café. Can you see where it is?

In the next place, you'll need to protect your head. Find this hard hat.

Can you find an artist who is drawing one of the things in the museum?

Some of the models light up or move when you press buttons or pull handles. Spot these things.

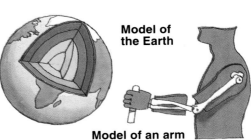

Model of the Earth

Model of an arm

The hospital

You've come to the hospital, where doctors and nurses are busy looking after the patients. Some people will stay in a ward until they are better, while others can go straight home once a doctor has treated them.

TOOL CHECKLIST

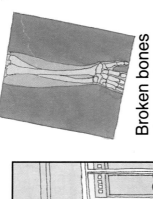

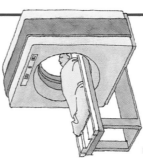

Broken bones show up on X-ray pictures. Spot nine.

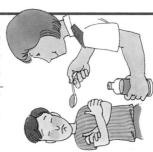

Doctors can use a scanner to see inside people's heads. Spot one.

Can you spot a boy who doesn't want to take his medicine?

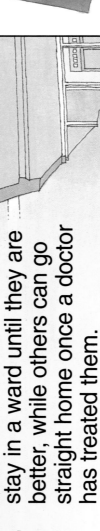

Mayor Maurice is making people laugh. Can you see where he is?

Doctors and nurses use stethoscopes to listen to people's insides. Can you find eight?

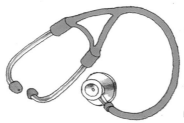

Visitors often bring bunches of flowers for patients. Can you spot 10?

Ambulances bring sick or injured people to the hospital. Spot one.

Plaster casts hold broken bones together until they heal. Spot 11 people who have them.

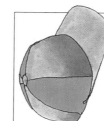

Next, you'll be outside. Find this hat to keep the sun off your face.

In the operating room, people wear special clothes to stop germs from spreading. Can you spot it?

Patients who can't eat are fed liquid food. It drips through tubes into their arms. Find 14 bags of liquid food.

Nurses work with the doctors and look after the patients. Spot 29 in their uniforms.

Many women come here to have their babies. Find 13 newborn babies.

Crutches help injured people to walk. Find eight pairs.

Patients in bed have their meals on a tray. Can you spot six trays of food?

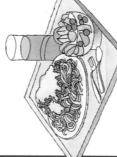

9

In the park

On a windy day, you can fly a kite. Spot nine.

Geese fly in to swim on the lake. Can you find 26?

Model boat

Paddle boat

The lake is full of **different** boats. Can you find seven of each of these?

Dogs **need lots of exercise. There's plenty of room for them to run around here.** Spot 12.

The park is a fun place to visit. You could play sports with your friends, go boating on the lake, or just laze around in the summer sunshine. It's good to get away from the noisy traffic and the dusty City streets.

The ice cream seller is very busy today. Can you find him?

Rolling along on in-line skates is a great way to enjoy the park. Spot 17 skaters.

Park wardens make sure the park is a safe place to visit. Find six.

TOOL CHECKLIST

Can you spot this toddler who is sitting on a swing in the playground?

Find 15 squirrels.

Gardeners look after the flowers and trees. Can you spot seven?

Can you find the fountain?

You'll be cheering people up in the next place. Find some balloons to give them.

People play games in the wide open spaces. Spot a frisbee and a soccer ball.

Joggers run slowly around the park to stay fit. Can you spot 18?

On the river

Mayor Maurice is waving at people. Spot him.

You use a paddle to move a kayak through the water. Find six.

Sailboats are blown along by the wind in their sails. Spot five.

Can you spot seven people who are fishing?

This old sailing ship is now a museum. Can you find it?

You've come to the deep, wide river which runs right through the City and on to the sea. It's very busy here with lots of different boats to look at. You can have parties and go on trips along the river on some of them.

You walk along a gangplank to get on board some boats. Can you spot one?

Artists paint pictures of the river for people to buy. Spot two.

The police patrol the river to make sure people are sailing safely. Spot a police boat.

TOOL CHECKLIST

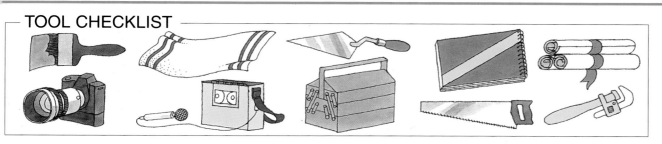

Can you spot 10 seagulls?

Life jackets keep you afloat if you fall into the water. Can you find 20?

Ducks fly in to swim around on the river. Spot 14.

Some people live on houseboats. Spot this one.

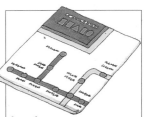

In the next place you'll need a map to help you get around. Can you spot one?

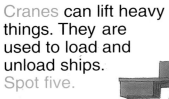

Cranes can lift heavy things. They are used to load and unload ships. Spot five.

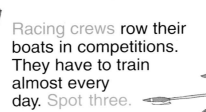

Racing crews row their boats in competitions. They have to train almost every day. Spot three.

At the school

Mayor Maurice can't find the right classroom. Can you spot him?

Teachers check the pupils' work in the staff room. Can you find it?

Can you spot 15 pupils who have put their hands up to ask or answer a question?

Clarinet

Violin

Flute

Pupils can learn to play a musical instrument. Find four of each of these.

Spot five televisions with video recorders.

You can learn many different things in this busy school. You could join in with an art class, learn a foreign language, or try a scientific experiment. You'll make lots of new friends as there are so many people to meet.

In the library, you can read or borrow books. Find the librarian who works there.

Each pupil has a locker to keep coats and bags in. Find 16 like this.

Can you spot this girl who is reading a funny poem to the rest of the class?

TOOL CHECKLIST

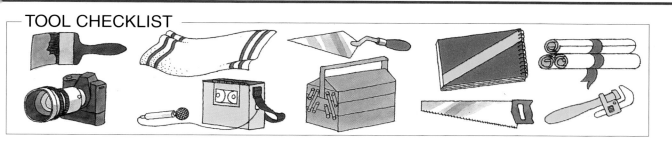

Globes show you where all the countries in the world are. Can you find four?

Woodwork

Pottery

Cooking

Can you spot where these different classes are happening?

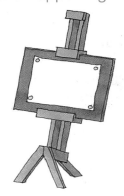

In art classes, you put your paper on an easel. Find nine like this.

You'll be doing lots of walking in the next place. Find these shoes.

You use Bunsen burners to heat up chemicals in science lessons. Spot six.

These things are used to play different sports. Can you spot six of each?

Tennis racket

Baseball bat

Soccer ball

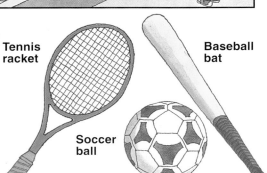

People use these machines to get money from the bank. Can you spot two?

Doll's house

Pandas

Trains

Find where these toys are for sale.

Find a girl having her feet measured so that her new shoes fit correctly.

You usually pay for things at a cash register. Can you spot six?

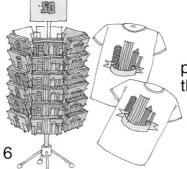

You can buy T-shirts and postcards with pictures of the City on the front. Find a place that sells them.

Buy birthday present.....30 minutes

Going shopping

Mayor Maurice has found something to buy. Can you spot him?

This shopping area is one of the liveliest parts of the City, with lots of different things for sale. You can look at the bright window displays or wander through the market. Wherever you go, there is plenty to buy.

Mannequins are models of people. They are used to display clothes. Spot 12.

Can you spot a thief who is stealing a pair of trousers?

TOOL CHECKLIST

Waiters and waitresses **serve food and drinks in the café.** Spot three of each.

The market stall holders use sets of scales to weigh out food. Find six.

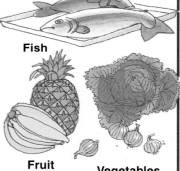

Spot 19 pigeons.

Fish

Fruit   **Vegetables**

Spot the market stalls which sell these things.

Next, you might be doing some cooking. Can you find this mixing bowl?

Musicians and entertainers earn money by performing for the shoppers. Spot each of these.

Guitarist   **Juggler**

Hanging baskets full of flowers decorate the street lamps. Spot 11.

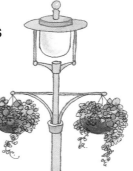

Underground

Mayor Maurice is in a hurry. Can you see him?

You can travel quickly by going under the City in a train. Spot two.

The roots of trees grow under the ground. Can you spot two trees?

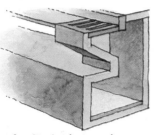

A drain is a pipe that carries rain-water away from the surface of the road. Spot two.

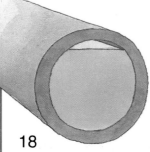

People working in tunnels often wear helmets with lamps. Can you spot three?

The City is such a crowded place, there are even things going on under the ground. You can go on a train inside a tunnel, or meet some of the people that work underground mending the pipes and cables.

Hundreds of water pipes carry water around the City and into buildings. Can you spot four?

Bulldozers clear away earth so pipes can be laid underground. Spot one.

The hotel has a busy kitchen which is under the ground. Find the chef.

Workers use pneumatic drills to dig up the road. Spot three.

Gas pipe fitter

Telephone engineer

Spot these people working underground.

Rats live in the tunnels and drains. Spot 12.

Electric cables carry power to all the buildings. Spot three sets of cables.

You'll be having fun in the next place. Find this inflatable rubber ring.

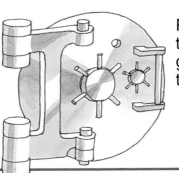

In the bank, money is stored in a safe room called a vault. Spot one.

People can park their cars in huge garages under the City. Spot four blue cars.

Building site

Dump trucks remove soil and rock from the building site. Spot two.

This man is in charge of all the building workers. Can you spot him in his office?

Welders use special tools to join metal parts of buildings together. Spot seven.

Find six wheelbarrows.

You've come to a huge building site. It's an exciting place to visit. There are lots of different vehicles and machines. It's amazing to think that in a few months' time, there will be a finished building here.

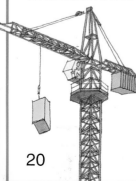

Tower cranes move heavy loads. They can be made taller as the building becomes higher. Spot two.

Workers go up and down in elevators. Can you find two?

Engineers use an instrument called an automatic level to check that the ground is flat. Spot two.

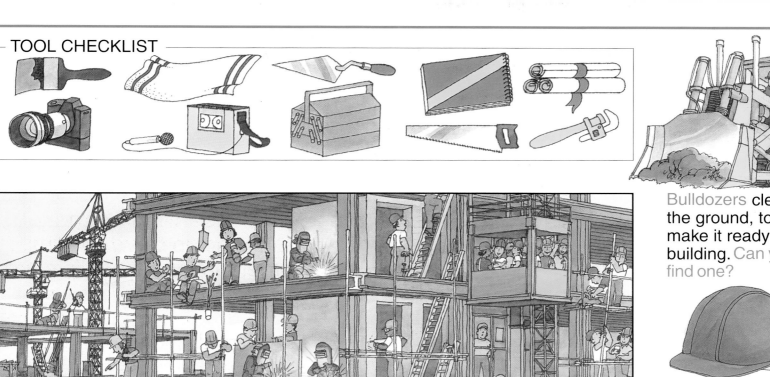

Bulldozers **clear** the ground, to make it ready for building. Can you find one?

The workers have to wear hard hats to protect their heads. Spot 18 red ones.

Concrete mixer trucks **bring** concrete to the building site. Can you find one?

Posters **show** people what the finished building will look like. Spot one.

In the next place, you'll have time to play. Can you spot this ball?

Workers who are far apart talk to each other using walkie-talkies. Spot eight.

Spot 11 ladders.

Piling rigs **drill holes** in the ground. Can you spot one?

On the street

Mayor Maurice is having a chat. Spot him.

Motorcycle messengers, called couriers, deliver urgent parcels. Spot nine.

You can buy hot snacks from food stands. Find four.

Can you find this statue of someone who lived in the City hundreds of years ago?

Satellite dishes pick up television and radio signals. Can you spot 10?

You have come to one of the busiest parts of the City. It is crammed full of people and traffic. There are also tall buildings called skyscrapers. Some people live here, while others travel here every day to work in the offices.

You can travel to different parts of the City by bus. Find three.

People put fuel in their cars from pumps at the service station. Find four.

Cyclists wear masks to keep out traffic fumes, and helmets to protect their heads. Spot 12.

To reach high windows, cleaners stand on a platform which hangs from the roof. Spot two.

Spot three helicopters.

Mosque

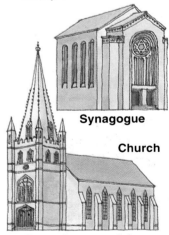

Synagogue

Church

People worship in different places, depending on their religion. Spot each of these.

A guide book will be useful in the next place. Can you spot one?

Policemen and policewomen keep the streets safe from crime. Spot two of each.

People put money in meters when they've parked their cars. Find 10.

Can you spot seven phone booths?

At the pool

Flippers help you to swim fast underwater. Can you spot 10 pairs?

Can you find **Chuck the carpenter** who built the wooden changing rooms?

Asha the architect drew plans which showed how to build the pool. Find her.

Armbands help you to float in the water. Can you spot 13 people wearing them?

Lucy the lifeguard organized the swimming lessons in the new pool. Can you find her?

You've arrived at the grand opening of the swimming pool. You can have lots of fun on the slides and in the water. All the people that you invited as you went around the City are here. Can you spot them?

Pippa the photographer took pictures of the pool for the City newspaper. Can you spot her?

When you've finished swimming, you'll need to dry yourself. Spot four red towels.

Can you spot Jack the journalist who wrote about the pool in the City newspaper?

24

Pete the planner **checked the plans for the pool before building began.** Spot him.

Can you spot 20 balloons?

Bob the builder **studied the plans and helped build the pool.** Can you spot him?

Sunglasses **protect your eyes from the sun.** Spot 17 people wearing them.

Pam the plumber **put in pipes to bring water to the swimming pool.** Find her.

Paul the painter **helped to paint the new pool.** Spot him.

Ellie the electrician **put in electrical wires so the pool could have lights and heating.** Find her.

Can you spot 15 sunbeds?

Mayor Maurice **is coming out of the changing rooms.** Can you see him?

City route

Follow the numbers on the map to see the route you should have taken on your trip around the City, and how you went from place to place.

KEY

1. Train station (page 4)
2. Shopping area (page 16)
3. School (page 14)
4. Street (page 22)
5. Museum (page 6)
6. Building site (page 20)
7. Park (page 10)
8. Hospital (page 8)
9. River (page 12)
10. Underground (page 18)
11. Swimming pool (page 24)

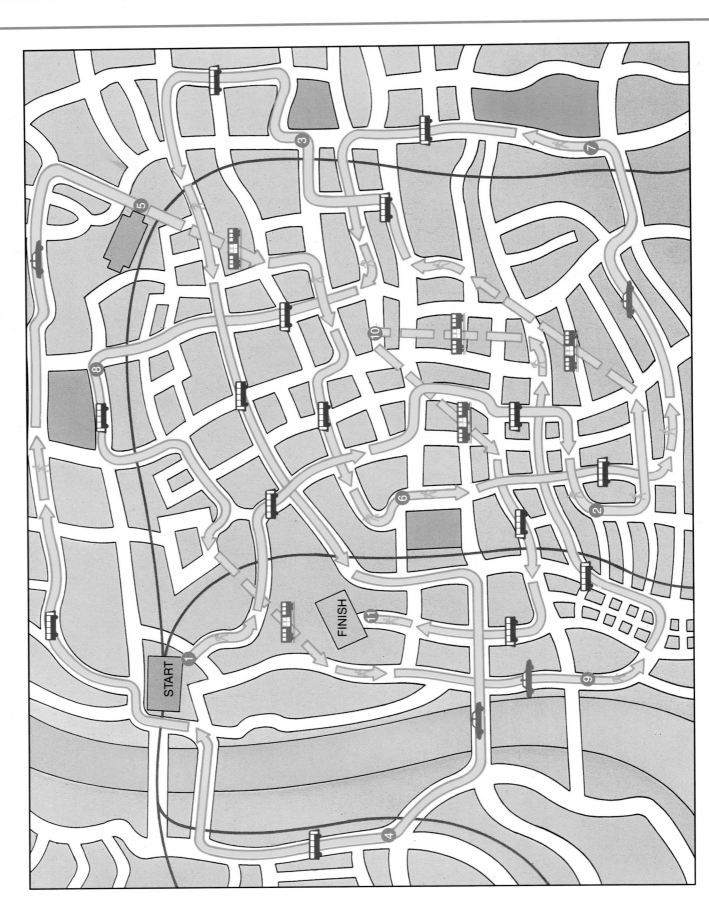

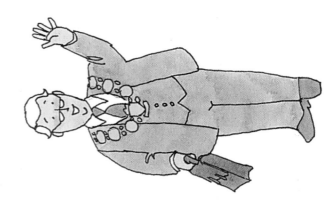

Extra puzzles

To do these puzzles, you'll need to look back through the book. If you get stuck, you'll find the answers on page 31.

1. Which of these machines do people use to get money from the bank?

A
B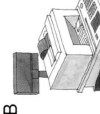
C
D
E
F

2. Which of these people delivers urgent parcels?

A
B
C
D
E
F

3. Which of these animals lives in drains and tunnels?

A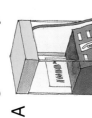
B
C
D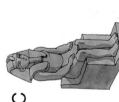
E
F

4. Which of these things is thousands of years old?

A
B
C
D
E
F

Journey times

At the beginning of the day, Mayor Maurice made a list of the things he had to do. This is what it said:

1. Meet station manager 8:00am–8:30am
2. Buy birthday present 9:05am–9:35am
3. Give talk to children 9:55am–10:45am
4. Business meeting 11:25am–12:00pm
5. Open the new display 12:45pm–1:45pm
6. Inspect new site 2:20pm–3:05pm
7. Relax in the park 3:35pm–4:05pm
8. Visit children's ward 4:35pm–5:35pm
9. Visit the party 6:15pm–6:45pm
10. Meet up with friends 7:10pm–7:40pm
11. Go to grand opening 8:00pm

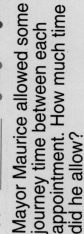

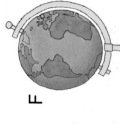

Mayor Maurice allowed some journey time between each appointment. How much time did he allow?

27

At the station 4-5

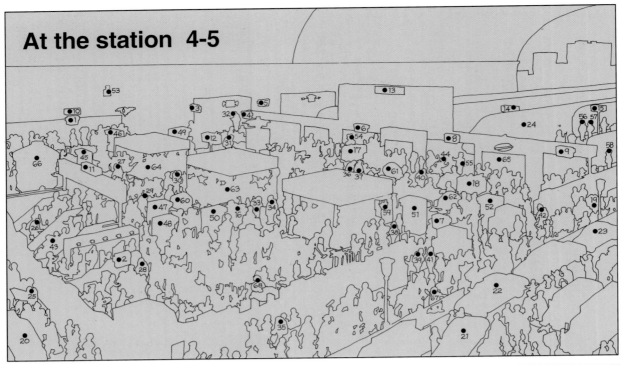

Screens
1 2 3 4 5 6
7 8 9
Clocks
10 11 12 13
14 15
Trolleys full of
mailbags
16 17 18 19
Taxis
20 21 22 23
High speed train
24
People with
backpacks
25 26 27 28 29
30 31 32 33 34
35 36 37 38 39
40 41 42
Down escalator
43
Man running to
catch train
44
Ticket machines
45 46 47 48 49
50 51 52
Conductors 53
54 55 56 57 58
Shopping bag
59
Cleaning
machines
60 61 62

Flowers
63
Magazines
64
Sandwiches
65
Information desk
66
Paul and his
paintbrush
67
Mayor Maurice
68

In the museum 6-7

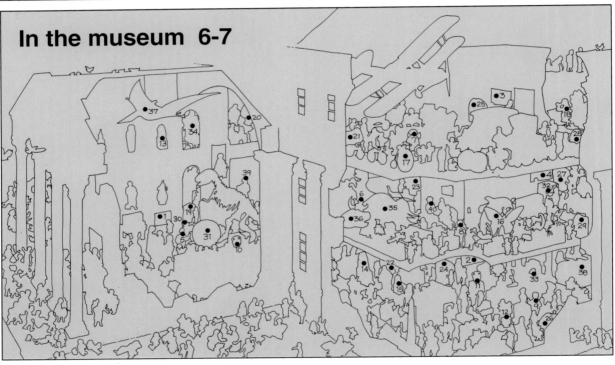

Museum plans
1 2 3 4
Guides
5 6 7 8 9
Greek vases
10 11 12
Egyptian
sculptures
13 14 15
Model butterfly
16
Penny Farthing
17
Curator using a
microscope
18
Telephones and
screens
19 20 21 22
23 24 25 26
27 28 29
Artist
30
Model Earth
31
Model arm
32
Hard hat
33
Café
34
Model
Triceratops
35

Model head of
Tyrannosaurus
rex
36
Model
Pteranodon
37
Mosaic
38
Asha and her
sketch pad
39
Mayor Maurice
40

The hospital 8-9

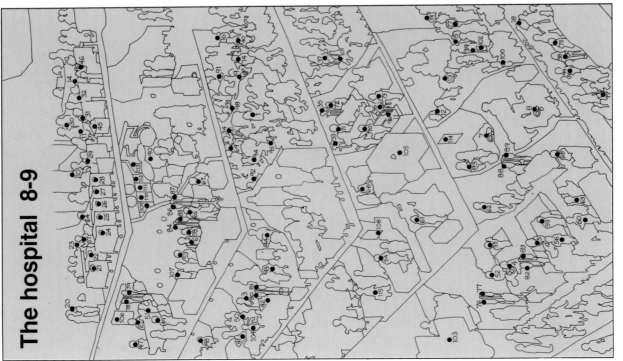

Mayor Maurice
1
Stethoscopes
2 3 4 5 6 7 8 9
Bunches of
flowers
10 11 12 13 14
15 16 17 18 19
Newborn babies
20 21 22 23 24
25 26 27 28 29
30 31 32
Pairs of crutches
33 34 35 36 37
38 39 40
Trays of food
41 42 43 44 45
46
Nurses
47 48 49 50 51
52 53 54 55 56
57 58 59 60 61
62 63 64 65 66
67 68 69 70 71
72 73 74 75
Bags of liquid
food
76 77 78 79 80
81 82 83 84 85
86 87 88 89
Operating room
90
Hat
91

Plaster casts
92 93 94 95 96
97 98 99 100
101 102
Ambulance
103
Boy who doesn't
want his
medicine
104
Scanner
105
X-ray pictures
106 107 108 109
110 111 112 113
114
Ellie and her
toolbox
115

In the park 10-11

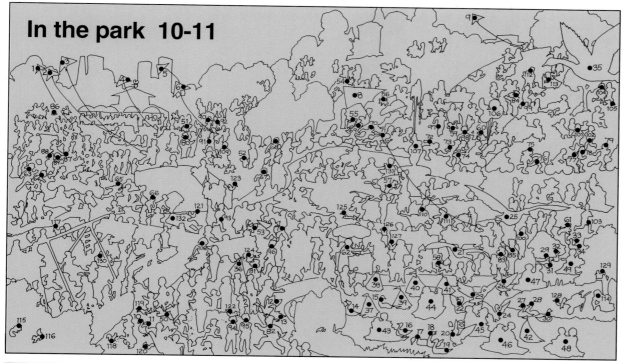

Kites
1 2 3 4 5 6 7
8 9
Geese
10 11 12 13 14
15 16 17 18 19
20 21 22 23 24
25 26 27 28 29
30 31 32 33 34
35
Model boats
36 37 38 39 40
41 42
Paddle boats
43 44 45 46 47
48 49
Dogs
50 51 52 53 54
55 56 57 58 59
60 61
Ice cream seller
62
Skaters
63 64 65 66 67
68 69 70 71 72
73 74 75 76 77
78 79
Park wardens
80 81 82 83 84
85
Frisbee
86
Soccer ball
87

Joggers
88 89 90 91 92
93 94 95 96 97
98 99 100 101
102 103 104 105
Balloons
106
Fountain
107
Gardeners
108 109 110 111
112 113 114
Squirrels
115 116 117 118
119 120 121 122
123 124 125 126
127 128 129
Toddler on swing
130
Jack and his
tape recorder
131
Mayor Maurice
132

On the river 12-13

Kayaks
1 2 3 4 5 6
Sailboats
7 8 9 10 11
People fishing
12 13 14 15 16
17 18
Old sailing ship
19
Gangplank
20
Artists
21 22
Police boat 23
Cranes
24 25 26 27 28
Racing crews
29 30 31
Map
32
Houseboat
33
Ducks
34 35 36 37 38
39 40 41 42 43
44 45 46 47
Life jackets
48 49 50 51 52
53 54 55 56 57
58 59 60 61 62
63 64 65 66 67
Seagulls
68 69 70 71 72
73 74 75 76 77

Chuck and his
saw
78
Mayor Maurice
79

At the school 14-15

Staff room
1
Pupils with
hands up
2 3 4 5 6 7 8 9
10 11 12 13 14
15 16
Flutes
17 18 19 20
Clarinets
21 22 23 24
Violins
25 26 27 28
Televisions with
video recorders
29 30 31 32 33
Librarian
34
Lockers
35 36 37 38 39
40 41 42 43 44
45 46 47 48 49
50
Girl reading a
funny poem
51
Bunsen burners
52 53 54 55 56
57
Tennis rackets
58 59 60 61 62
63
Soccer balls 64
65 66 67 68 69

Baseball bats
70 71 72 73 74
75
Shoes
76
Easels
77 78 79 80 81
82 83 84 85
Cooking class
86
Pottery class
87
Woodwork class
88
Globes
89 90 91 92
Pete and his
plans
93
Mayor Maurice
94

Going shopping 16-17

Machines
1 2
Doll's house
3
Toy pandas
4
Toy trains
5
Girl having her
feet measured
6
Cash registers
7 8 9 10 11 12
T-shirts and
postcards
13
Mannequins
14 15 16 17 18
19 20 21 22 23
24 25
Thief
26
Guitarist
27
Juggler
28
Street lamps
29 30 31 32 33
34 35 36 37 38
39
Mixing bowl
40
Vegetable stall
41

Fruit stall
42
Fish stall
43
Pigeons
44 45 46 47 48
49 50 51 52 53
54 55 56 57 58
59 60 61 62
Sets of scales
63 64 65 66 67
68
Waiters
69 70 71
Waitresses
72 73 74
Lucy and her
towel
75
Mayor Maurice
76

Underground 18-19

Trains
1 2
Trees
3 4
Drains
5 6
Helmets with
lamps
7 8 9
Water pipes
10 11 12 13
Bulldozer
14
Chef
15
Vault
16
Blue cars
17 18 19 20
Inflatable rubber
ring
21
Sets of electric
cables
22 23 24
Rats
25 26 27 28 29
30 31 32 33 34
35 36
Telephone
engineer
37
Gas pipe fitter
38

Pneumatic drills
39 40 41
Pam and her
wrench
42
Mayor Maurice
43

Building site 20-21

Dump trucks
1 2
Man in charge
3
Welders
4 5 6 7 8 9 10
Wheelbarrows 11
12 13 14 15 16
Tower cranes
17 18
Elevators
19 20
Automatic levels
21 22
Walkie-talkies
23 24 25 26 27
28 29 30
Ladders 31 32
33 34 35 36 37
38 39 40 41
Piling rig
42
Ball
43
Poster
44
Concrete mixer
truck
45
Red hard hats
46 47 48 49 50
51 52 53 54 55
56 57 58 59 60
61 62 63

Bulldozer
64
Bob and his
trowel
65
Mayor Maurice
66

On the street 22-23

Couriers
1 2 3 4 5
6 7 8 9
Food stands
10 11 12 13
Statue
14
Satellite dishes
15 16 17 18 19
20 21 22 23 24
Buses
25 26 27
Pumps
28 29 30 31
Cyclists
32 33 34 35 36
37 38 39 40 41
42 43
Policemen
44 45
Policewomen
46 47
Meters
48 49 50 51 52
53 54 55 56 57
Phone booths
58 59 60 61 62
63 64
Guide book
65
Church
66
Synagogue
67

Mosque
68
Helicopters
69 70 71
Platforms
72 73
Pippa and her camera
74
Mayor Maurice
75

At the pool 24-25

Flippers
1 2 3 4 5
6 7 8 9 10
Chuck the carpenter
11
Asha the architect
12
Armbands
13 14 15 16 17
18 19 20 21 22
23 24 25
Pippa the photographer
26
Red towels
27 28 29 30
Jack the journalist
31
Ellie the electrician
32
Sunbeds
33 34 35 36 37
38 39 40 41 42
43 44 45 46 47
Mayor Maurice
48
Paul the painter
49
Pam the plumber
50

Sunglasses
51 52 53 54 55
56 57 58 59 60
61 62 63 64 65
66 67
Bob the builder
68
Balloons
69 70 71 72 73
74 75 76 77 78
79 80 81 82 83
84 85 86 87 88
Pete the planner
89
Lucy the lifeguard
90

Answers to Extra puzzles on page 27

1. D   2. B   3. F   4. C

Journey times

1 – 2: 35 minutes   6 – 7:   30 minutes

2 – 3: 20 minutes   7 – 8:   30 minutes

3 – 4: 40 minutes   8 – 9:   40 minutes

4 – 5: 45 minutes   9 – 10:   25 minutes

5 – 6: 35 minutes   10 – 11: 20 minutes

Acknowledgements

The publishers would like to thank the following organizations and individuals for their help in the preparation of this book:

pages 4 – 5: The Railways Board, Euston House, 24 Eversholt Street, PO Box 100, London, NW1 1DZ, England

pages 6 – 7: Ben Spencer, Museum Educator

pages 8 – 9: Jenny Thompson, Pediatric Nurse Specialist

pages 10 – 11: Royal Parks Agency, The Old Police House, Hyde Park, London, W2 2UH, England

pages 12 – 13: Paul Dykes, Environment Agency, Kingsmeadow House, Kingsmeadow Road, Reading, Berkshire, RG1 8DQ, England

pages 14 – 15: Timothy Crockatt

pages 16 – 17: City of Westminster, Department of Planning and Environment, Westminster City Hall, 64 Victoria Street, London, SW1E 6QP, England

pages 18 – 19: Roy C. Browne, Client Director (Highways), City of Westminster, Department of Planning and Environment, Westminster City Hall, 64 Victoria Street, London, SW1E 6QP, England

pages 20 – 21: Alan Clarkson, Balfour Beatty Civil Engineering Ltd., 7 Mayday Road, Thornton Heath, Surrey, CR7 7XA, England

pages 22 – 23: City of Westminster, Department of Planning and Environment, Westminster City Hall, 64 Victoria Street, London, SW1E 6QP, England

Artwork on pages 28-31 by Edwina Hannam

Map artwork on pages 2 and 26 by Mark Franklin

First published in 1997 by Usborne Publishing Ltd, Usborne House, 83-85 Saffron Hill, London, EC1N 8RT. www.usborne.com Copyright © 2003, 1997 Usborne Publishing Ltd.

The name Usborne and the devices ♀ ⊕ are Trademarks of Usborne Publishing Ltd. All rights reserved. No part of this publication may be reproduced, stored in a retrieval system or transmitted in any form or by any means, electronic, mechanical, photocopying, recording, or otherwise, without previous permission of the publisher. UE. First published in America March, 1998. Printed in Spain.